SHARK SEARCH

In Search of
Bull Sharks

Whitney Hopper

PowerKiDS
press

New York

Published in 2016 by The Rosen Publishing Group, Inc.
29 East 21st Street, New York, NY 10010

First Edition

Editor: Caitie McAneney
Book Design: Mickey Harmon

Cataloging-in-Publication Data

Hopper, Whitney.
In search of bull sharks / by Whitney Hopper.
p. cm. — (Shark search)
Includes index.
ISBN 978-1-5081-4335-2 (pbk.)
ISBN 978-1-5081-4336-9 (6-pack)
ISBN 978-1-5081-4337-6 (library binding)
1. Bull shark — Juvenile literature. I. Hopper, Whitney. II. Title.
QL638.95 H856 2016
597.3'4—d23

Manufactured in the United States of America

CPSIA Compliance Information: Batch #BW16PK: For Further Information contact Rosen Publishing, New York, New York at 1-800-237-9932

Contents

Bloodthirsty Bull Shark

What's the most **dangerous** shark in the world? You may think it's the huge great white shark. However, many **experts** believe the bloodthirsty bull shark is even more dangerous.

What makes bull sharks so scary? They're **aggressive** animals that eat nearly anything they can catch. They hunt along coastlines where many people surf and swim. Unlike most sharks, bull sharks can even swim in freshwater, where people least expect them.

Bull sharks don't want to eat people. However, if they cross your path, they won't think twice about attacking!

The Hunter's Habitat

There are some sharks you'll never meet. That's because they live in deep ocean water. However, the bull shark likes water that's shallow, or not deep. It likes to hunt its **prey** close to shore. It's found in coastal waters all over the world.

Like most sharks, the bull shark lives in salt water. In the United States, bull sharks are commonly found along the Atlantic coast. Swimmers in the Gulf of Mexico also have to be on the lookout for this wild hunter.

Bull sharks live and hunt where many fish are available.

Freshwater Foes

Most people think they're safe from sharks in rivers. However, bull sharks often swim up rivers and streams—even the mighty Mississippi River! They hunt prey that other sharks can't get to.

How can bull sharks survive in freshwater? They still need salt to survive, like other sharks. However, they have special **glands** near their tail that help them hold salt. Their kidneys also work differently than those of other sharks. This helps them stay in freshwater.

In the Central American country of Nicaragua, people have seen bull sharks swimming upstream against strong river currents to reach Lake Nicaragua.

Lake Nicaragua

Bull Shark Body

Bull sharks get their name from their square **snout**, which looks somewhat like a bull's. They're known to hit their prey with this snout. Like the bull, this shark is also very aggressive. It has a body built for the hunt.

Bull sharks are much smaller than their scary cousin, the great white. Females grow to around 11 feet (3.4 m), while males grow to around 7 feet (2.1 m). They have a thick, strong body. Their long pectoral, or side, fins help them swim quickly.

You can **identify** a bull shark by the shape of its snout and its coloring. Bull sharks are gray on top and white on their underside.

blunt snout

dorsal fin

caudal fin

pectoral fins

Amazing Senses

Like all sharks, bull sharks have special senses that help them live and hunt in water. They have a great sense of smell and can pick up on very small amounts of blood in water from far away. They have eyes that can see very well in low lighting, which helps them as they swim through **murky** water.

Bull sharks also have **receptors** that help them sense movement in the water. Other receptors help them pick up on the electric fields given off by prey.

If there's prey around, a bull shark's senses will find it.

13

Predator and Prey

With its supersenses, strong body, and many sharp teeth, the bull shark is a predator that can't be beat. These sharks aren't picky when it comes to prey, so any creature nearby is in trouble.

Bull sharks hunt fish and even other sharks. They'll attack ocean **mammals**, such as dolphins. They'll eat sea birds that fly too close to the water. Bull sharks will even catch turtles and crack their shells for a treat!

Bull sharks are on the hunt day and night.

The Life of a Bull Shark

Bull sharks are solitary animals, which means they live and hunt alone. However, they do come together to mate, or make babies.

A mother bull shark usually gives birth to her babies, or pups, in spring or summer. She goes to an **estuary** to have her babies. Each mother can have between one and 13 pups. She leaves them as soon as they're born. They already have teeth, and they're born ready to hunt prey.

Unlike most fish, mother bull sharks carry live pups inside of them. The pups are born ready to swim.

Bull Sharks Attack!

The three sharks most likely to attack humans are great whites, tiger sharks, and bull sharks. The thing that makes bull sharks so dangerous is that they can swim into freshwater where people don't expect them.

In India, near the Bay of Bengal, many people fish while standing in water. For years, villagers had suffered many attacks by a huge, unknown fish. Experts went to the village and found that bull sharks had been swimming up the river and were likely responsible for the attacks.

Possibly the earliest recorded shark attack in North America was the fault of a bull shark. In 1642, a man named Anthony Van Corlaer was killed by a bull shark while trying to swim across the Hudson River.

19

Safe Swimming

Fortunately, there are only around 16 shark attacks every year in the United States. Most of those attacks aren't deadly, but people have gotten nasty bites and even lost body parts.

How can you stay safe? Never swim in murky water. You want to be able to see if a shark is swimming around. Never swim alone. Stay close to shore, and only swim in areas that are watched by a lifeguard. Stay away from large schools of fish—those are the shark's targets.

If you hurt yourself and are bleeding, don't go into the water. Also, don't splash around too much. A bull shark can mistake you for easy prey!

Shark Bites!

 Bull sharks have been found as far inland as 2,500 miles (4,023.4 km) up the Amazon River.

 Bull sharks can live to be around 16 years old if they're female and 12 years old if they're male.

 Some bull sharks live in lakes, such as Lake Nicaragua.

 Female bull sharks grow larger than males.

 Bull sharks have multiple rows of sharp, triangle-shaped teeth. The back rows of teeth move forward when the front teeth become worn down or broken.

 Many bull sharks don't **migrate** far, but the South American bull shark migrates around 2,300 miles (3,700 km) each season.

Saving the Bull Shark

Right now, bull sharks aren't in danger of dying out. However, their numbers are possibly decreasing because they're overfished. Also, their **habitats** are taken away when people build along the coast. The coasts are becoming increasingly polluted, which can make sharks sick and reduce the number of prey that live in the area.

We have a responsibility to keep this awesome hunter around for a long time. Bull sharks may be killers, but they can be admired from a distance!

Glossary

aggressive: Showing a readiness to attack.

dangerous: Unsafe.

estuary: An area where the ocean's tide meets a river.

expert: Someone who has a special skill or knowledge.

gland: A body part that produces something that helps with a bodily function.

habitat: The natural home for plants, animals, and other living things.

identify: To tell what something is.

mammal: A warm-blooded animal that has a backbone and hair, breathes air, and feeds milk to its young.

migrate: To move from one area to another for feeding or having babies.

murky: Very dark or foggy.

prey: An animal hunted by other animals for food.

receptor: A nerve ending that senses changes in light, temperature, or pressure, and makes the body react in a certain way.

snout: An animal's nose and mouth.

Index

Websites

Due to the changing nature of Internet links, PowerKids Press has developed an online list of websites related to the subject of this book. This site is updated regularly. Please use this link to access the list: www.powerkidslinks.com/search/bull